THE SCOTTISH HIGHLANDS

THE SCOTTISH HIGHLANDS

PHOTOGRAPHS BY DAVID PATERSON

TEXT BY

DOROTHY DUNNETT

AND ALASTAIR DUNNETT

MAINSTREAM
PUBLISHING

MAINSTREAM PUBLISHING COMPANY
(EDINBURGH) LTD
7 Albany Street
Edinburgh EH1 3UG
ISBN I 85158 1499 (cloth)

British Library Cataloguing in Publication Data

Dunnett, Dorothy, *1923*
The Scottish Highlands.
1. Scotland. Highlands. Description & Travel.
I. Title. II. Dunnett, Alastair 914.11'504858
ISBN 1-85158-149-9

Design by James Hutcheson
Typeset in Berthold Bembo
by Artwork Associates, Edinburgh
Origination by Marshall Thompson Ltd, Edinburgh
Printed and bound in Singapore by Toppan

For Mayumi and Sean

CONTENTS

INTRODUCTION
by Alastair Dunnett

Y OU'LL HARDLY FIND A PART OF THE KNOWN WORLD WHERE THERE ISN'T a local and national zeal for the overwhelming beauty of the surroundings and pride in national achievements and traditions. Scotland got a flying start in this cult, chiefly with the works of Sir Walter Scott whose output, starting about the turn of the last century, inspired the romantic movement that endured for all of the 19th century and in many ways is still going on. A Scottish borderer in heart and head and by no means a Highlander, he saw the Highlands as a place of heroic mysticism and enchantment, peopled by fierce, independent folk who had defied the legions of Rome and the terror of the Vikings, imposing a heroic concept of themselves on neighbours and enemies and, in gentler times, yielding a remote dignity of style to those who cared to venture among them.

Scott saw the Scottish Highlands as a superb setting for his own ideas of story-telling and of true romance and he entered into it with superb zest. First came – after his fling with border poetry and legend – the series of great epics that made his name, *The Lay of the Last Minstrel, The Lady of the Lake, The Lord of the Isles.* Any one of these one-man dramas, with all the enduring and beautiful lyrics embedded in them, could still be performed by a talented solo artist in a way to move even a modern audience. At the time, their impact was tremendous and they flew abroad in translations to a world eager to hear of the mysterious Highlands, all the more so since the works had come out of the embattled island of Britain, standing alone, as usual, in defiance of an implacable enemy who was determined to conquer the world.

For years Napoleon had been rampaging up and down Europe and into Africa, capturing countries and laying them under his will; but his great prize had still eluded him, so that the epics came from a Britain moved to extraordinary heroism by defiance of the aggressor and the determination to remain independent. Before long Napoleon had been put down at Waterloo and that fear was over, so that there came a boom of the freedom to rejoice and to fare forth and be seen as British adventurers, and also to move into the remote parts of our own country where it was seemly to assume we had derived our roots of staunchness. Into this scene Scott led with his novels, and they told the same story, raging across the same irresistible theme and location. To be sure he made some literary excursions into the fringes of the Continent and even England, but his main setting became and remained Scotland and especially the Highlands.

Scott had not been entirely the inventor of all of this new-found enthusiasm for the Highlands. He had closely succeeded Robert Burns, whose genius in lyric poetry and satire on the natural scene far outstripped his own, but who had also made statements that had been valid and repeated ever since Galgacus. And even before that there had been the dim figure of James Macpherson who had produced the Ossian sagas, and got no thanks for it from such sour critics as Samuel Johnson. It was well rewarded otherwise. Macpherson's stories remain, in origin, something of a mystery, but there were undoubted fragments of these great tales around in the Highlands at the time and they were being recounted often in oral tale-telling. They too had set, in an early form, the romantic mood and it perhaps wasn't much comfort to the embattled regiments of the British resistance to learn that Napoleon had a French edition which he carried around with him everywhere and that he no doubt refreshed himself with tales of Celtic conquest.

Sir Walter Scott, therefore, laid the foundations for the early British tourist trade. People poured into the Highlands, especially when they knew it was clear he had had the royal blessings. Queen Victoria dowered the Scottish scenes with her presence and ready yielding to the romantic notions of her own ancestors. Hotels and roads were made and were busy. Cotters and farmers turned to the tourist supply industry. Wealthy merchants and entrepreneurs bought tracts of wild land and made demesnes. The pattern was set that can be seen today, because what all these visitors got was value for money and effort.

The Highlands may fairly be counted as the area between a line drawn roughly from Glasgow to Aberdeen. Everything north and west of that qualifies as the Highlands except for a few non-Celtic fringes here and there. In this small area the drama of the topography is absolutely staggering – mountain, moor, glen and flood, spouting or trickling rivers or shallows, abounding waterfalls, sudden aspects of trees and rich valleys and wild moorland and hills and crags that look enormous in the strange light, and vales that are mysterious and silent. To this paradise of scene and atmosphere come a multitude of tourists to be readily absorbed in the spacious acres and miles of our welcoming land. Many of them are canny folk who live far into the south of England, poor souls, and take two or three precious weeks roving the roads and walking the hills and storing memories for their long winters beside the Thames. To these incomers, in the last

50 or 60 years, have been added hordes of our own young folk whose fathers and grandfathers had been dragged from the glens into the industrial south of prosperous Scotland around the Clyde and the Lothian works. By some impulse that spread among them like a fever they set out to find the hills of their forefolk and got to know Scotland, travelling as it were on a shoestring, kilt-wearing, many of them; others took to the crags with rope and axe and reached an Alpine standard. You see them everywhere now and some of the rock faces near main roads, if you study them, are twitching with their ropes and perilous ascents, or their tents are hidden and glowing in some benevolent valley and you hear their voices and songs chiming in the evening. These sons and daughters of industry bear, many of them, the old clan names and they have gone back to find their roots and to rejoice in their modest and proud past.

There is another aspect of this urban Scottish search for roots which has to be understood and even tolerated. It gave rise, as many another tradition has done, to a certain almost bogus invention of the past which hardly existed and which gratifies in some way the Highland city dweller and perhaps even the unwary tourist. Songs abound, and pawky references which have no authenticity. Things about "shielings in the glen", whereas there never were shielings in the glen, the shielings being the little summertime huts high in the hills where the cattle were taken, mainly by the women and the children, to feed on the high growth while the crops developed in the fields around the villages below. You will hear sturdy wights singing of "marching through the heather", whereas the one thing you cannot do with heather is march through it. And there is many another false premise in these well-meaning sentiments. But there are still lots of bonnie lasses, and the dancing goes on, and many a song and story, and a dram or two, and good talk and friendship, and a welcome for the understanding visitor.

Edinburgh,
January 1988.

THE SCOTTISH HIGHLANDS

by Dorothy Dunnett

THE SOUTHERN HIGHLANDS

CONSIDERING PERTHSHIRE, IT HAS OFTEN OCCURRED TO ME THAT I probably owe my marriage to Rob Roy MacGregor. A day among the romantic wild hills of Balquhidder, visiting the grave of the Highlands' best-known robber baron, and thence climbing barefoot up to the great waterfall that drops like a curtain from the mountain behind, sealed the fate of a teenage romance. Before that, I knew little of the Highlands, although Pitlochry, with its dramatic peaks, lush afforestation (and its theatre) had long appealed to my English mother, and I knew the softer parts of Perthshire quite well, with its sensible farms and wide fish-filled rivers and lochs. I was taken as a child to see the oldest yew in the world at Fortingall, where Pontius Pilate was said to have been born; and sketched the bridge at Aberfeldy, the finest built by the English General Wade when constructing the network of roads which were meant to subdue the Jacobite Highlands.

With Alastair and later the family, the explorations became considerably tougher. But set amid the prodigious green landscape were places to be picked for their history, and accessible to those without tackety boots and binoculars. As a writer, I paid many a professional call (and more for the love of it) on the grey stone city of Perth itself, once the capital of all Scottish commons and chivalry; and on the mound of Scone near it. Here on the Moot Hill was the traditional home of the Stone of Destiny, now at Westminster Abbey. The mound itself, so they say, was created from earth brought to the spot by the vassal chieftains to honour their leige lord; and here, in the 8th century, the Pictish King Nectan was held to embrace the customs of the church of Rome. Never subdued by the Romans, the Picts fell in time to the conquering Irish gaels who called themselves Scots, and Scone of the melodious shields yielded its throne to Kenneth mac Alpin.

The present handsome palace stands on the site of earlier buildings, but there is no trace now of the monastery where Duncan and Macbeth were both installed on the throne. Dunkeld Cathedral, just to the north, dates back in part to the 12th century, but there, too, under its hallowed and elegant roof, one must imagine the earlier days when Duncan's father was abbot, and the whole abbey of Dunkeld was put to the flames.

One doesn't need to imagine how the Tay Valley looked in Victorian times: it has been painted over and over by – surprisingly – the esteemed and urbane Sir John Millais, whose second wife, Effie, had parents living in Perthshire. To sustain him while painting in snow, he complained "he drank enough whisky and water to make an ordinary man quite giddy; but without feeling it". Reinforcement is, of course, a necessity when painting in Scotland. It is fortunate that the means are never too far to seek; so long as you remember which is the turpentine flask and which is the water.

South of Pitlochry (since we've mentioned Macbeth) is Birnam, site of the mysterious wood which disguised Malcolm's troops and fulfilled the prophecy of disaster in Shakespeare's play. There is no reason to think it really happened, but you can stand on this hill and gaze across the 12 miles to the hill fort at Dunsinane and imagine it did.

Certainly armies have tramped through these passes many times. North of Pitlochry is the Pass of Killiecrankie where, 300 years ago, the last wolf in Perthshire was killed, and the Battle of Killiecrankie was fought in which an army of Highlanders, outnumbered two to one, defeated William of Orange's general. Despite the victory, the Highlanders' leader was to die from a wound through his breastplate. His name was John Graham of Claverhouse, Viscount Dundee; and the songs and legends about Bonny Dundee can be heard to this day (this household in particular has a large Scottish repertoire). And further north still are the forests of Atholl and the Duke's vast seat, Blair Castle. In his ancestors' warlike history, the least remembered fact had perhaps the greatest importance for the landscape around him – it was a Duke of Atholl in 1728 who introduced to Scotland the lovely larch tree whose bright tips speckle the hillsides in spring.

That is the merest sampling of Perthshire: in itself enough to explore half a lifetime. Argyll you would never know in several lifetimes, it is so wild and ancient and mysterious, so broken by sea inlets and curious islands. It is my husband's calf country; and he sent me there, an innocent of 17 on a bicycle, with an oil-painting box strapped to the saddle, on an apparently disinterested recommendation to stay at Lochgilphead, and make the acquaintance of a dear second cousin in Castleton (who knew very well what was afoot, if I did not). I remember the archaic quality of the small, rounded hills; the old graveyards; the great primitive boulders with their unreadable cup and ring marks; the Standing Stones – the first of many I was to see in the years to follow.

It is regal country. You would know it even before you set eyes on the wide flat marsh that lies between Loch Fyne and the sea, in the midst of which rears the rock of Dunadd, with its Ogam script, its incised boar, and its naked print cut in the summit into which chosen kings placed a foot, standing facing the far peaks of Cruachan during the ritual of inauguration. From the signs, the land about Dunadd has been inhabited for thousands of years, but the land reached its great days between 500 and 800 AD when, according to legend, the first Christian kings in Britain were enthroned on that same Stone of Destiny which later found its way to Scone – and to London.

Among its many beautiful places, Argyll holds also two glens of sorrow. The story of Glencoe, and the massacre that took place there one snowy night in 1692 is not spoken of lightly today by either Campbells or Macdonalds, much as the American Civil War is still an uncivil topic in partisan households. Because of the nature and scale of its rock, Glencoe even today has a ferocity somewhere about it. The only way to shake it off is to climb it, as many do, replacing fear with delight.

The other vale is Glen Etive, and its sorrow lies in the exquisite and ancient story of white-handed Deirdre who fled with her lover Naoise, son of Uisneach, to build her bower of ferns in the glen. Tempted to go back to Ireland, she is trapped by King Conchobar, rival of Naoise, and finds herself bereft, as a magic sea raised by his enemy rushes over the land and drowns her beloved and his brave brothers. The lament of Deirdre for her lost happiness in the sweet glens of Alba has been made and remade in music . . . *From the hillside calls the cuckoo, and methinks I hear it still . . .* but never fails to echo the anguish.

Above all the powerful names associated with Argyll stands that of the Duke, whose treasure-packed turreted home at Inveraray Castle with its great wall of weapons replaces a 15th-century castle built a mile to the south, with its village. An early Campbell married the sister of King Robert the Bruce, and succeeding generations were to show themselves expert ministers to the government in authority – sometimes admired for it by their fellow Highlanders, sometimes roundly condemned. When King James IV asked his Campbell Chancellor to resettle the lands of the Lord of the Isles, the resulting plantations of fair-haired, blue-eyed Campbells spread their influence throughout Argyll, mainland and islands.

Stewarts also have their place in Argyll; some less royal than others. Appin, north of Loch Etive, was the site of a famous 18th-century killing, when a Campbell was murdered from ambush and a Stewart was hanged for the crime, having been tried at Inveraray by a judge and jury of Campbells. I've heard the case argued yet round the table, especially if there's a Stewart feeling cantankerous.

The builder of Castle Stalker, in the same district, was said to be another Stewart – Duncan Stewart of Appin, who had the chance of entertaining James IV when that same king was putting his west Highland subjects to rights. In later, more careless days, the castle was lost through a wager.

Central Argyll is not without a reputation for strong-minded inhabitants. Robert Burns was in no two minds about them. On the window of the Argyll Hotel in Inveraray he inscribed his opinion:

There's naething here but Hielan' pride,
An' Hieland scab, and hunger;
If Providence has sent me here,
'Twere surely in His anger.

Dr. Johnson, on the other hand, was "very kindly entertained by the Duke of Argyll at his splendid seat" at Inveraray in 1773, and even found a "tolerable inn" in the fishing village of Oban. Boswell House now stands on the site of the inn, and Oban is the great hotel and touring centre of the west, from which the enchanted islands are visited by sailing-dinghy, cruise ship or yacht.

Alastair introduced me to the matter of sailing in the early days of my athletic instruction, explaining the principles with the greatest lucidity: "If you shove the tiller hard left, the boat will move right. And vice versa." He also taught me never to take my eye off the burgee: a thing hard to do when you are wearing spectacles and it is raining. I have fried in bathing suits on board big boats and small, and frozen inside a full set of stiff yellow oilskins. But among all the joys and disasters of seamanship, nothing is quite so sobering as to get caught in a storm in a motor-cruiser with a waterlogged engine, and have to be towed into Oban harbour by Grannie Spence (the saint and monitor of all naval accidents) under the smug gaze of all one's seafaring friends.

The little islands clinging to the coast south of Oban, with their big neighbours Jura and Islay are easily reached; but under the green, cheerful blanket of streams and grazings and farms there is present once more that whiff of the occult which presses so heavily over Dunadd. The Celtic church long ago, taught by the hermits of the Egyptian desert, sought solitude for its contemplation, and clung to small islands and rocks which still bear their chapels, or what was left of them after the Viking raiders began to find their way there, and steal cattle and burn huts and take away cooking pots and crucifixes and silver. There are beehive cells as well as a fort on the Garvellach islands, in the sea-path from Ireland to Oban. The name, Garbh Eilach, means the rough, rocky place; and Eilach an Naoimh, the Rock of the Saints, is the particular island where St. Brendan the Voyager (they say) founded his small Christian community. There, huts, ruined chapel and gravestones show how long the island has been steeped in mysteries.

Closer to Oban are Luing, Seil and Easdale, famous for their quarries of thin blue stacked slate, which roofed the reconstruction of Iona Abbey. There, too, is the Cuan Sound, that innocent passage of water that, at the wrong state of the tide, can turn itself into a dizzying race of swerving currents and watery saucers.

Its big brother is, of course, Corryvreckan, the great whirlpool which lies between the islands of Jura and Scarba. I have anchored beside it, off Jura, and sailed safely on with a watchful eye on the tide. But the roar of the pool in full spate can be heard far away, and a small boat caught there would be in trouble. Wendy Hiller, playing the heroine caught in such a way in this very maelstrom was filmed by Michael Powell for the climax of *I Know Where I'm Going*. She was wearing Alastair's yellow oilskin, battered, worn and much loved, because friend Michael thought it would make a better contrast to Roger Livesey's blacks. Probably due to the oilskin, she escaped unscathed.

Lastly, we are reminded of God's island, Gigha; on the face of it a douce piece of land like the rest, but like Rhum, owning a double identity because of the works of a recent landowner. The family who introduced Horlicks to cure the night starvation of the world also introduced to the island of Gigha the rare and exotic rhododendrons and other flowers that fill the walled garden at Achamore House, once looked upon by an equally rare collection of fine jade within.

It was at Gigha that one of the ubiquitous folding pocket-balances of Viking times was discovered, proving that businessmen of the past, too, have come here to buy and to sell; although generally seeking something more material than peace, tranquillity, and the beneficent warmth of the Gulf Stream.

THE CENTRAL HIGHLANDS

I ALWAYS THINK OF INVERNESS AS A CLEAR, COLD, LOGICAL CITY, PLACED under wide skies on the edge of a broad, shining river, with all its history freeze-packed under the soil instead of thick in the air, as in the west of the Celts. They say, and rightly, that the best English in the British Isles is spoken there. The accent is a distillation of all the races that once have met in that spot: the musical Gaelic of the west, combined with the force and the clarity of Norman and Norse.

It is the terminal point of the two great military roads built by General Wade, stretching from Dunkeld and Fort William, and was once the centre of a land famed for its timber and salmon. Gun dogs and fishing rods still debouch from its sleeper trains annually. Nothing remains of its earliest days but a 14th-century church tower, and the fragments of a 13th-century priory. If King Macbeth had one of his several halls there – and he probably had – it would have been made of timber, and was not on the present castle mound. Nor is it too likely that King Duncan met his death there, as Shakespeare would have it. Of two possible sites mentioned by the earliest chroniclers, Inverness is the easier to pronounce and the less likely to be correct.

When (according to Adamnan) St. Columba visited the 6th-century Pictish king Brude, the Pictish settlement may have been on the hill of Craig Phadrig, two miles west of Inverness.

Inverness itself, of course, stands on the river of the same name, which leads into the loch famous (since the 1930s) for its monstrous inhabitant. The legend is, however, earlier than that: dating back to the same St. Adamnan, who refers in his writings to a much earlier monster. It is possible. The loch is 24 miles long and in parts over 700 feet deep, and has never been known to freeze over. It is not the fault of its tropical climate. Sailing from east coast to west on a sharp early spring day, a hot breakfast below is well begun with a half-pint of freshly squeezed juice from oranges chilled by the night air on deck. Then, at every lock is the gossip, with the shoremen and other seafarers, before being let loose to sail another broad sheet, as loch links with loch through the Highlands. Small boys and dogs are natural lovers of lock gates and their mechanism: ours have pushed back many a gate, striving manfully in their small wellingtons. Sailing down the Caledonian Canal, from Inverness through Loch Lochy to Fort William is as good as coming from Caithness by train, stopping at every small, busy station. And to the north are all the fine glens to explore and to fish in, of which Glen Garry, clothed in trees and kindly to peculiar visitors arriving on horseback, sticks most firmly in my memory.

The tragedies in the past of Inverness-shire tend to be stark and vicious and recorded in pen and ink, not cut in pictures on stone, or painted into prayer books or missals. In 1746 the Duke of Cumberland defeated and scattered the army of Prince Charles Edward Stuart on the field of Culloden in the last land battle ever fought here in Britain. The only stones here incised are those still to be seen, marking the mass graves of the dead of each clan. Bidden to spare none of the wounded, the English cavalry sought out and massacred all they could find: the protesting provost of Inverness was kicked downstairs for his temerity. The place of the battle is today one of solemn and touching remembrance, and a fitting memorial.

Stories crowd round the escape of the Prince, as they cling to his every appearance in Scotland. Between the Great Glen and Skye is Loch Morar, whose blue-green infinite depths and white sands the prince reached in his wanderings. There Lord Lovat, his equivocal follower, was captured and later beheaded. At nearby Glenfinnan, where once the Prince, full of hope, raised his standard, there is both a monument and a visitors' centre in which you can see how it all began and how, after Culloden, it ended.

Fort William, at the southern end of the Caledonian Canal is a handy centre, but there is no trace now of the fort, first built by General Monk and subsequently improved upon in an effort to quell all those disorderly Highlanders. This is Lochaber, Clan Cameron country. Cameron of Locheil was one of the Prince's most loyal supporters and the whole area, with its vent to the Western Isles and to Ireland and France has always had historic importance. When the historian Boece invented "Banquho, thane of Lochaber" as Macbeth's cousin and henchman, it was to indicate that the King's future rival was a powerful man. If he hadn't been spurious, I should have had an excuse to return to Lochaber and seize him by the hairs. I still return, none the less.

This is the land mass that thrust up Ben Nevis – the highest mountain in Britain, and amazingly easy to climb. So they tell me. I have never been up it. The height of my achievement in that direction was to walk to the top of Goat Fell in Arran, with small children jumping and leaping before me. The last time I tried it, I needed ten-minute pauses between every three steps.

This is not to say that I dislike winter pursuits: quite the reverse. I long enjoyed the experience of skating badly in the company of almost anybody, although the great Scottish sport of curling escaped me. Living in Edinburgh, which has the biggest dry-ski slope in Europe, it seemed ridiculous to send one's children to learn, and never know the pleasures of proper skiing in the Cairngorms where – recently in my non-existent sporting career – a great skiing centre had been created at Aviemore. Alas, the menfolk in the household proved to be natural learners, while the solitary female ended with no skills whatever, and a bent thumb from the matting which objected to car doors for two months. I have no sense of balance, my mother says. Alastair's mother told him he had no sense of proportion. They were both right.

It was from the region of Aviemore and Kingussie (centre of the district of Badenoch) that Alastair and I set out on the first of our summertime travels by garron. His must be the expert word on those journeys through mountain and forest, which were meant to follow the old roads of General Wade, but more often diverted us on to hard single-passing-place roads because of the boggy mud of the tracks. We had, I remember, hail in June on one of those excursions: we dressed as if for a small yacht, with towels round our necks, and crushed oats in our saddlebags next to our pyjamas.

I remember few trips so hilarious, or so spectacular. We were at one with the landscape. Rolling deer paid no heed to us. We watched eagles, and breathed in the smells of the horses, of peat and heather and garlic and honey, and pitied tourists passing us in warm, comfortable buses with the windows all steamed up round the wipe-marks. Also, because garrons are built something like tables, it is quite hard to fall off one, even when it is moving.

Wonderful Badenoch rolls and rages in the middle of an area bounded by the Atholl, the Grampian and the Monadhliath mountains. The Wolf of Badenoch had his base in the middle of this territory, in the place now marked by the ruins of Ruthven Barracks (built in 1718 to keep the Highlanders in check). Not one of nature's sophisticates, the Wolf was the brother of King Robert II and distinguished himself by burning Elgin Cathedral.

Near at hand, surprisingly, is the house built by James Macpherson of "Ossian" fame, whose work caused more to burn than even Elgin cathedral. Or perhaps not surprisingly, for legends abound, from that of the Old Man who guards the tombs of the Shaws in Rothiemurcus to the Red-Handed Spectre who challenges all comers close to Loch Morlich, but who has never yet been seen by those who come to sail and camp today at this prettiest of small lochs.

Winding from Aviemore to the sea south of Elgin is, of course, the River Spey, that great torrent from which fat salmon have been caught and salted and sent in their barrels to the Baltic for as long as records tell. Its other historic harvest was timber; felled in Glenmore and Rothiemurcus and sent over the rapids in rafts to the Moray Firth, far to the east, in a way every Canadian lumberjack would recognise.

The Spey flows through Grant country. Castle Grant stands on its banks, and the family's town, Grantown-on-Spey, founded by Sir James Grant in 1776, opposite the road to Braemar. Stately hotels were built, to which came summer visitors to enjoy the healthy, pine-laden air – my parents among them. Later, I came to examine its history. The name early appears as Le Grant, and its first holder must have been a large man. Exploring, for my own nefarious purposes, the Grants of Aberdeen – from the same stem – I came across a John le Grant who, in 1453, had helped defend Constantinople against the Turks' final attack. He was an engineer, as many a Grant has been since. So was my father. I hope the original John le Grant will not blame me for adopting him.

The Speyside of today, it must be said, has something to offer which the 15th century didn't yet know. Alastair is the connoisseur (of course) of all matters to do with malt whisky. I will merely say that a drive from distillery to distillery, with the warm and comforting smell of the mash in the air, is a pleasant way of seeing some exceptionally beautiful country. And you can have your dram once you are safely at home.

THE ISLANDS

A SUNLIT DAY IN THE HIGHLANDS IS BETTER THAN THE BEST DAY IN MOST other places. There is nothing anywhere in the world as breathtaking as the Hebridean sea under blue summer skies, with the green, white-stranded isles lying on it.

Such days come now and then. There are times of wet and cold also. There are days of wind, and days of mysterious mist. There are days of Olympian drama, when Atlantic rollers crash on the rocks, and storm-clouds tower, and sunsets lower and flare like rivers of lava. But sometimes the sun remembers where it has been, and the lark sings, and the smell of flowers fills the air, and seals lie comatose on the rocks or each other, or peer out from the waters like umbrella handles.

The beaches of the Hebrides are made of shell sand, white as soap-flakes, and stretching for miles and miles empty. If the fine weather stayed the strands would be thronged with promenades on them. But, like the Islands of Youth, the Hebrides find their high summer by chance, for a week or a day or – unbelievably – sometimes for a month or more at a time; and, if you are there, you bless yourself and the fates; and if you had to leave for the city the day before, you sigh and say, "Maybe next time". Well, maybe.

I first discovered Mull and Iona through sailing in small boats with Alastair. It was for me a pilgrimage in any case, following in the tracks of the quest by canoe he tells of elsewhere. He also told me the stories of all the places we were passing: Lady Rock, at the mouth of the Sound of Mull, where a Maclean chieftain of old left his wife at low tide to drown. (Mind the buoys, to see which side to pass it.) On the south cliff, the stronghold of Duart, the fortalice of the chiefs of Clan Maclean, and their comfortable, wind-seared Highland home to this day. On the northern shore, the ruins of Ardtornish Castle, an early home of the Lords of the Isles. Then, at the end of the green, winding sound, the inlet that leads into the crowded, bustling anchorage of Tobermory, with its ring of taverns and shops and the big hotel perched on the cliff-top.

There are always friends there, with a story to tell (just then I said, "Dougie, we'd better get the second warp out . . .") and the ones who are not there will be, no doubt, in the bar. The bonhomie of west coast amateur sailors arises from natural spirits, and also from relief, for the sea outside Mull requires courage and stamina from its sons, not to mention skill and a water-fast bottom.

To attain Iona, you must sail west and south, passing (or calling to dip into) the delights of the Treshnish Isles and their companion orchis-starred islands of Ulva, Gometra and Staffa. Nearing Staffa, the air is filled with cassetted Mendelssohn, as every cruiser brings out its recording of *Fingal's Cave* and plays it through to the cormorants. The Cave itself is one of the places where I plotted a murder. I remember well standing beside its black organ-pipe rocks, memorising the swelling boom of the sea as it burst at the far end of the dark, water-filled cavern, sucking the gravel noisily back in receding.

From there, Iona is close, although the mile that separates it from the south of Mull is fierce with currents, and it is possible to stand on one side, almost within hailing distance, and yet be unable to cross. Perhaps because of its isolation it lays upon all who come a sense of ultimate peace and tranquillity. It has a few gentle hills, but is largely flat, with a pebbled beach to the west on which you may still pick up fragments of green Iona marble. The expanse of air and sea all about it seems to diminish all sound, so that men are insignificant. What remains are the grey broken stones of early Christian worship; the restored cathedral; the carved and knotted stone crosses, and the natural beauties of the wind and the grasses and the lapis blue and jade green of clear water lying over white sand.

It has a long history. There were settlements here before the 6th century, when St. Columba sailed with 12 men from Ireland and chose this spot – the first out of sight of his home – on which to found his small monastery. From there he carried Christianity to the Picts of the mainland and Iona remained a centre of worship until Viking raids forced the abbot and monks to flee to Ireland

and Kells. The *Book of Kells,* treasure of Trinity College, may well have been started in Iona. In return, it must be admitted that the glorious claim for an unbroken line of buried royalty must be suspect. Only after the robber raids ceased, and the monastic settlement was restored to its glory would proper rites and protection be possible. But still the tombs of kings and chieftains may be seen, from times that are early enough to be remarkable.

Sailing from Iona to Rhum's devilish, mist-savaged mountains, a sensitive soul might well wish St. Columba were with him. But on Rhum today – and it is the size of Jersey – can be found nothing more deadly than several herds of red deer sporting ear-tags, and a number of cheerful members of the Nature Conservancy, who use Rhum for their researches. The island has breeding cliffs of guillemots, puffins, fulmars and razorbills – familiar sights in nearly all the small islands – but its unique possession is the vast red sandstone edifice of Kinloch Castle, built in 1900 by the Bulloughs of Lancashire when Rhum was their private estate. The interior in its heyday was filled with immense and valuable pieces of furniture, porcelain and trophies brought home from China in the family yacht. The mahogany baths and willow-pattern lavatories are there still. Alastair speaks of other implications. I shall only admit that a few years ago, I was guilty of committing a murder in one of its baths, and employing its unusual organ as a clue in a singularly tortuous plot, for which I have not so far been arrested.

A real and multiple killing blackens the name of the island of Eigg nearby, with its curious crest. There, in a 16th-century feud, several hundred men, women and children of the Clan Macdonald were suffocated in their hiding place by a landing party of MacLeods from Skye. The story is told in the *Lord of the Isles* by Sir Walter Scott, who visited the cave where they died, and found and brought home a skull.

The island of Skye, of course, has been fought over by the Madonalds, the Mackinnons and the MacLeods ever since the days of the Vikings and the Lords of the Isles. Lord Macdonald (and his lady of the mouth-watering recipes) still lives in the south of the island. The chief of the MacLeods occupies Dunvegan Castle, the seat on the west which has been theirs since at least 1200. Inside, framed on the wall, is the Fairy Flag, faint and fragmented, made of 7th-century Syrian or Rhodian silk. Legend says that it has the power three times to save the MacLeods from destruction. It has been twice unfurled.

Letters from Prince Charles Edward Stuart are to be found in the Castle, for it was to Skye that his wanderings brought him after his flight from Culloden.

Finding that government vessels were threatening his movements in the Outer Hebrides, his friends decided to convey him somehow to the east. Flora Macdonald, then aged 24, and keeping house in South Uist, had a mother who was not only determined to rescue the prince, but managed to obtain the connivance of her second husband, who happened to be the very captain of militia who was supposed to be hunting for him. The plan was to send her daughter Flora to Skye in the company of a manservant and a maid. As Betty Burke, the maid, the prince made an awkward, long-striding figure, but did achieve his escape. The story goes that Miss Flora had to dress him herself in petticoat, bonnet and gown after he had stripped himself to his breeches. When she objected that a pistol under his clothes would betray him, he parried with an objection she was unlikely to question: "Indeed, Miss, if we shall happen with any that will go so narrowly to work in searching, they will certainly discover me at any rate." He left Flora Macdonald at Portree, and never met her again. Nor was he ever betrayed, although there was a price of £30,000 on his head.

From Portree, Princes Charles was rowed to Raasay, the green island that closes the mouth of the bay. North of Raasay is South Rona, a small isle deserted except by the birds and the seals and sundry yachtsmen like ourselves, as Alastair tells. Myself, I exploited the place (yet again) as an ideal scene for fictitious skulduggery. Will no place remain safe?

From here to the Outer Isles is a good sail, and can be rough or idyllic, according to the mood of the Blue Men of the Minch, who will arise from the waters and challenge you with a half-finished verse, which you must complete to their satisfaction if you are to survive.

The Outer Isles, too, are haunted by the ill-fated Prince, and I have trodden the white sands of Eriskay (the place of the love-lilt) scanning the machair for signs of the small, white flowering plant they say was put there by the Prince's own hands when he first set foot on Scottish soil. Eriskay, of course, is famous not only for flowers but for the most alcoholic shipwreck of all time, when the *S.S. Politican* sank with her cargo of export whisky in the first years of the last war, to be celebrated by Compton Mackenzie and film-maker Alexander Mackendrick in the hilarious *Whisky Galore.* Belated bottles recently retrieved have been wryly spoken of, but Alastair who was (of course) at its earliest tasting declared the stuff nectar.

I have been, in my time, strenuously introduced to many places in the Long Islands, whether by small yacht or cruise ship or cargo boat. Of glories now past, there are few memories finer than those of ten-day trips in a spare double cabin aboard one of the smaller vessels of the great Clan MacBrayne, delivering crates and sacks (and friends, and bottles) from island to island. These were long days at sea, with Jimmy Shand thundering forth from the radio and plates of food like Ben Nevis sliding to and fro in the mess room, while the jokes and gossip of the islands passed around with the drams. To honour the Sabbath, it was usual to tie up on the Saturday, and set sail again at a minute past midnight on Sunday. So, if you were in Lochboisdale, you could walk across to the sand and machair at Daliburgh, and bathe in the icy clear Atlantic. If you were in Tarbert, Harris, you could fish in the lochs, or hire a car to take you north to Stornoway where (I was early informed) there was the only Woolworth's in the British Isles where the assistants addressed you in Gaelic.

Lewis has, of course, its own Stonehenge. The avenue and ring of tall monoliths stand at Callanish, just 16 miles west of Stornoway. A great cairn lowers in the centre, and one wonders, walking towards it, fenced by stones, what took place there under the stars, or the sun, or the moon. But pre-history has been grudging in yielding its secrets. They are solemn totems, these stones, whether you meet them in Orkney or Malta or Brittany, or in those parts of Scotland where they stand, sometimes alone, as dumb as the strange symbol stones of the Picts. It has always seemed to me that those in Lewis and Orkney especially have a power endowed by their setting that is quite another thing from the familiar, much-abused ring of the south.

A delicacy in Lewis is the flesh of guga, young salted gannet, made into a paste and eaten on finger-toast with whatever liquid you favour. A quarter of the world's population of gannets lives on St. Kilda, the group of isles which stands far out into the Atlantic, with nothing but sea between it and America. Loneliest of Britain's Atlantic islands, St. Kilda is on the same latitude as the south part of Greenland. Its rock-needles are famous: Stac an Armin, at 627 feet, is the highest sea stack in Britain, and among the curiosities of St Kilda wildlife are a wren and a mouse which are unique to the islands.

There is now an army outstation there, but the last true inhabitants left in 1930 when life became too hard to sustain. Before that, the nimblefooted St. Kildans climbed the rock sea-stacks barefoot, taking the gannets as they nested there in their thousands. They climbed, too, down to the fulmar ledges, where the birds gave them oil for their lamps and feathers for pillows. The birds are still there, hissing if you pass them incautiously, and every visiting ship is given the spectacle of a blanket of gannets lifting to darken the sky, and then plummeting down, black-tipped wings folded like fins, as they shear the water for fish, or for refuse.

The other resource of the St. Kildans were the Soay sheep – small animals, agile as goats, and fleeced in every shade from cocoa to black. They still breed among the rocks and turf and flowers that top the frightening cliffs, and you will see a soldier sometimes sitting in spring in the sunshine, with his boots apart, and a small tugging black lamb between them, taking its orphan measure from a stoutly held bottle.

As in the Long Island, there are fairy tales here – they will show you the house of an Amazon – and tales of the Vikings who long roved in these parts. And sometimes – for all the army can do – St. Kilda is lost altogether, cut off by air and by sea, with a storm whirling about it that may be St. Kilda's alone, for those dramatic peaks springing from the grey sea have no neighbours, and make their own weather. But the seals have no objection or the gannets.

THE NORTH AND WEST HIGHLANDS

EVERYONE CALLED DUNNETT COMES FROM CAITHNESS. DUNNETTS NOW living in the United States (and there are quite a few) prefer to pronounce the name as if it were French, but it is more likely to be Gaelic in origin. Three hundred years ago it was spelt in all sorts of ways, including "Dinnit". This is the way it is pronounced still in the place of its origin, which is the most northerly point of mainland Britain, beside the soaring red cliff known as Dunnet Head. A few centuries ago, the same headland called itself Windy Knowe. Later, presumably, it adopted the name of its inhabitants, rather than the other way round – a matter for which present Dunnetts must all be mildly grateful.

Dunnet Head *is* windy, too. I climbed it the other day with elder son Ninian, and we have photographs of each other, arms outspread, leaning on the wind at an angle of 45 precarious degrees, with the sea crashing away 400 feet below. From 1601 the famous map-maker Timothy Pont was minister in Dunnet church, and must have found the view from the headlands of Caithness a perfect cartographer's dream.

He was an incomer. Examining the natives, the only thing I would swear to (having met quite a few Dunnetts) is that they are not descended from either Vikings or the late Norman landowners who became the lords of this region. Dunnetts are primarily Picts: the small, dark early settlers who used the defensive sea-towers, 2,000 years old, still to be seen through all this territory. Pure Picts the Dunnetts are not; for their cousins the Mowats have exactly the same cast of visage: fair skin, brown eyes and black curly hair, and the Mowats *did* come from Normandy. Proving that the powerful little Pict, of the pictorial stones and fine silverwork and shrewd eye for defences, had furthermore a set of genes fit to conquer his conquerors.

From Dunnet Head you can view the hills and flat islands of Orkney, separated by the Pentland (Pictland) Firth, a stretch of water that has seen more sea battles than most, and can still drown the unwary yachtsman with its fierce tides and races – the flood at full moon runs at ten miles an hour. The Icelandic sagas, written 700 years ago, tell how the leaders of the north fought for supremacy in these waters, then the highway from Norway to Ireland and the Welsh coast and France, and later the passage from Scandinavia to the North American continent.

In the days I was then writing of, the north was under Norse dominion, and the Earls of Orkney ruled the whole of Caithness and Sutherland – which simply means the south lands of Caithness. Thurso, on the north coast, has been a fisher-settlement since Viking times, and was once the chief port for Scottish-Scandinavian trading. Its harbour at Scrabster still sees the passage of ferry and cargo boats to and from Orkney. From here, too, flagstone used to be shipped all over the world from the quarries round Thurso, and its thin, blue-grey wafers can be observed even yet crossing fields as a superior substitute for scarce wooden fencing.

By the 18th century, Thurso was being described as "a neat little fashionable town" – a bland assessment that makes no allowance for the particular brand of sour Caithness humour that any Dunnett would recognise. *Cape Wrath* was the popular name for the windiest corner in town, and the land next to the kirkyard was referred to as *Gravesend:* a punning allusion to visiting fishing-boats from that exotic port. Witchburning is supposed to be connected with a certain flat stone which had the property (they said) of remaining visible, no matter what men might do to it. There is a tale of a local grieve who once deposited 20 cartloads of earth on the spot and, two days later, the stone was clearly on view again. Given the winds of Caithness, I'm not sceptical.

Thurso is Sinclair country. Known in the north since at least the 14th century, the family became local landowners through the marriage of a daughter of Earl Malise of Caithness and Orkney with a noble baron of Roslin whose ancestors came from Saint-Clair-sur-Elle in Normandy. Thurso Castle, as presently seen, is a Sinclair stronghold. There, too, is an early dry-stone broch and the ruins of the Bishop's Palace, as well as the remains of the church of St. Peter whose tower-base may be as old as the 12th-century chapel of St. Margaret in the Castle of Edinburgh. And on the hill above Thurso you can see where Earl Thorfinn's castle once stood, until it was thrown down by King William the Lion. Thorfinn's great fleet of flat-bottomed galleys must often have called at the river-mouth, and lain beached where the sand-yachtsmen now run on the magnificent two-mile stretch of pure sand that lies below Dunnet Head.

There are later castles, or ruins of them, all round the coast, and traces of Viking longhouses – there is one in Freswick which had the ash of its longfire still in place when discovered. Lambaborg (now Bucholie Castle) was built in the 12th century by a famous Norse pirate Sweyn, and lies just south of the famous John o'Groats beach on the Pentland Firth. Knives and keys have been found in such sites, and combs and bracelets of the kind common too in the Western Isles and Scandinavia. Indeed, the coast is the glory of Caithness, where the battering seas have broken the steep red cliffs into needles and stacks, ridged with the nesting-places of thousands of auks and puffins and skuas, and favoured by exotic migrants. But of course it is not, nowadays, only a matter of scenery. More important than immigrant birds are immigrant technical folk who have changed the nature of the small talk in the well-stocked hostelries of Thurso. And at Wick (known to the saga-writers) you can do what the Vikings never did, and warm your hands at the molten glass rods of the Caithness Glass factory, which welcomes the curious.

The great fishing days of Wick were those of the herring, but there are white-fish boats still in the harbour designed by Telford and improved by the grandfather of Robert Louis Stevenson. There is also, a little way off, a clifftop fragment of castle – one of two in the neighbourhood. Old Wick, one of the oldest stone castles in Scotland, was owned in the 14th century by another Norman, Sir Reginald de Cheyne. A fight over a will saw the end of the other: Girnigoe Castle, a 15th-century seat of the Sinclairs which was claimed by a Campbell. The struggle, in 1690, was the first in which firearms were locally discharged in anger, and the Sinclair prevailed in the contest, although the fortalice lost. A Caithnessman is a dour fellow to cross.

All the north of Scotland contains the mixed blood of the Scandinavian lords who settled there, and intermarried with the local Picts and Scots. Time and history saw to it that the eastern side of the country kept alive its Norse connections when those of the west and south were being more aptly replaced by the Gaelic culture of the Isles and of Ireland. In the

13th century the lands of Sutherland were given to Hugh of Moray, a man this time of Flemish descent, whose family seem to have intermarried with the old house of Moray from which the Mackay chiefs are thought to spring. Dunrobin Castle, begun in the same century and still the chief Sutherland stronghold, was named after Robert, the Sutherland Earl who married a daughter of the Wolf of Badenoch.

The family have had shrewd sons as well as turbulent ones. It was the 13th Earl of Sutherland who had the first coalpits sunk at Brora in 1598. But the great statue of the first Duke on Beinn Bhraggie commemorates the English husband of Elizabeth, Countess of Sutherland. It was his wrongheaded policies of reform which led to the cruel emptying of the glens called the Clearances – a matter over which correspondents of douce Scottish newspapers are sometimes to be found quarrelling bitterly to this day.

Under the shadow of the statue is Golspie, with its sandy beach; and south of that is Loch Fleet, the seawater bight which leads to the glen of the same name. The causeway at the head of the loch was raised by Telford. North of Brora, on the way to the fishing township of Helmsdale, you find yourself at the entrance to the misty Glen Loth. A monument at the foot of the glen records the killing, in 1700, of the last wolf in Sutherland. To which the only possible rejoinder is – no comment.

Strathnaver, the north-west corner of northern Scotland, is Mackay country. It contains Cape Wrath and other places of curious name, such as Bettyhill (named after Elizabeth, first Duchess of Sutherland) and Tongue. (Teenage son, telephoning a few years ago to report (unhurt) the spectacular crash of (my) car: "Mum? Are you sitting down? I'm in some place – I'll spell it – called Tongue".) Tongue (from Norse *tunga*, a tongue of land) was kind to him; and as a result the two of us possess a special affection for both Tongue and Ben Loyal, whose sunlit snow we had first seen together that windy day on the headland at Dunnet.

Ben Loyal, Ben Hope and all the striding mountainous giants of the north and the west are part of Alastair's personal history and not of mine, although I have passed them admiringly on wheels and on water. I have yet to see lovely Loch Eriboll, of which the Brahan Seer recorded that one day it would witness the end of a war. It probably overlooked quite a few skirmishes in its time, but credence had to wait until the end of the Second World War, when German submarines chose to come there to surrender.

Further south, in Ross-shire, I first traversed the easier paths on pony-back, insecure as ever, on a trek with Alastair from Spean Bridge to Kinlochewe, during which I made my first acquaintance with the sweet bay at Shieldaig. From there, we took the shore route to Torridon on a finely kept right-of-way which is now a road, and busier by far than it was when our ponies brushed through it, leading us up to the moorlands proper and through the woods bordering the lochside, far from traffic. Further on was the spectacle of the silver quartzite pow of Ben Eighe sparkling against the blue sky, with the magenta of bellheather on its slopes. Worse than a foray of clansmen were the midges that greeted us and the ponies as the breeze dropped at dusk, but I remember still our lodging in quiet Kinlochewe; the deep blue of Loch Maree visited on the following day, and the wrench with which we parted with it all at the Achnasheen railhead.

Viewed from the sea, the shapes and colours are quite as compelling: the adventure of a different kind. Sailing up the broad expanse of Loch Ewe, which only a neck separates from the long valley filled by Loch Maree, it is possible to drop anchor, as once we did, and visit the tropical gardens marvellously preserved here at Inverewe by the freakish warmth of the current they call the Gulf Stream.

Planted more than 100 years ago by Osgood Mackenzie, the garden was created by love and by labour – the soil was brought here in creels to relieve the black treeless peat of the peninsula. It is now protected by fir, pine and eucalyptus, within which is a flowering expanse of wall garden and pond, rock garden and grove, massed azalea thickets and walks lined with rare rhododendrons. South African lilies flourish here, and New Zealand jasmine; palm trees and Australian tree ferns, a Chinese handkerchief tree and – most surprising survivor of all – a bed of giant forget-me-not, nurtured on seaweed and herring-fry in place of the shark flesh of its native New Zealand. The National Trust for Scotland now own the garden and have made of it a bower of pleasure within the greater treasure of the wild land around it which, through every tint of light and turn of climate and atmosphere refreshes all those who move within it, whether they come to write or to remember; to paint with brush or the sensitive eye of the lens.

THE SOUTHERN HIGHLANDS

Text by Alastair Dunnett Photographs by David Paterson

ARGYLL AND PERTHSHIRE OCCUPY MOST OF THE SOUTHERN HIGHLANDS of Scotland and, without stepping into another county, you can walk from the Atlantic to the North Sea on these two alone. The eastern boundary of Argyll marches with the western boundary of Perthshire in a north/south line which is followed almost exactly by the railway track which bears the Highland Line trains between Glasgow and Fort William.

Argyll is a sea county, with long fjords fingering in from the south-west, where the gales come from. The Vikings never really got much of a foothold here, so that the place-names remain Gaelic, unlike those of the north and the farther west islands where the names tend to be Scandinavian, descriptive of landmarks as suited a sea-roving people. Here in the southern Highlands are two of our favourite glens – Glen Lyon in Perthshire and Glen Orchy in Argyll. From the dam in Glen Lyon you can walk through a track that leads you round the south shoulder of Ben Doran and across both the railway line and the road, from which it is a step into Glen Orchy. Ben Doran, which dominates the pass where the road and rail tracks go, is a conical hill of real beauty.

Argyll belongs to the sea, and no part of it is more than 12 miles from salt water. If you are looking at size, it is the second-largest county in Scotland. Parts of it, such as Kintyre, are further south than parts of England, and it has innumerable inhabited islands off its coast, with car and passenger services running to many of them. There are small towns too, such as Dunoon, where the famous "Thousand Pipers" march every year; and Oban, which anticipated modern tourism last century by calling itself "The Charing Cross of the Highlands". There is even an American colony north of Dunoon on the sea inlet called the Holy Loch, the home of Polaris submarines.

But, chiefly, Argyll is a county of villages, or even simply valleys with scattered dwellings. Standing in many of these glens, you can see dotted all over the landscape the white small houses of the crofters who make a meagre living from hard agricultural labour. Their patches of land are small, with rough hill outruns for sheep whose wool and mutton are prized. It is a way of life that tends to induce a sense of personal peace and dignity, but it often requires that the chief breadwinner of the household has to seek part-time employment in some other area for the sake of a cash income.

The great industry used to be herring fishing; a business sadly subject to fluctuations of supply and of market, and the uncertain tides of fortune for those who live by the sea. Its original home was Loch Fyne, whose kippers, or smoked herrings, have come back (like the Highland lobster elsewhere) into the favour of gourmets. The herring fishing nowadays is centred mainly on Tarbert, a dramatic port in Loch Fyne, with a fine secluded harbour and houses rising back up the hills from the sea's very edge. When you see the name Tarbert in Highland maps and signposts, you can expect to find there an isthmus joining one sea with another through a narrow strip of land. Tarbert has a ruined castle which was once a stronghold of King Robert the Bruce who regained independence for Scotland at the Battle of Bannockburn and demonstrated through such strongholds his intention of keeping it. At one time, every village in Loch Fyne contributed its seafaring skills to the herring-fishing, and I watched in my boyhood, herring boats, crewed by three or four men each, sail out from Inveraray, Cairndow, Furnace, Minard, Ardrishaig, Otter Ferry and others. It's a pity that, in the name of centralisation, all this should have gone. Something has been lost.

The outstanding possession of Argyll, however, is quite different. It is something that must be called, quite simply, the landscape. Here there are no precipitous crags, as in Cairngorm and Skye. The hills are rounded and tend to be low, and are sometimes so green that you could imagine a ploughman could walk over the top of them and down again. The hillsides are steep, however; and great torrents of water come foaming down in the frequent cloudbursts over the hills, leaving a countryside marked by white spouts and waterfalls.

This was the country that the young descendants of clan people first discovered as they made a breakout from the industrial lowlands in the early 1920s. Ill-clad, ill-shod, and with only the remotest instincts for open country and the hills, they were to be seen in these times standing at road-ends on the outskirts of Glasgow and the other industrial and decayed cities, seeking hitch-hikes into the clan country. Alastair Borthwick has written splendidly about these pioneering tramps, some of whom went on to Alpine standards of mountaineering, rock climbing and ski-ing. In the course of time the wealthier among them – the term is comparative – bought or made or restored small boats and sought around the coasts and into the farthest heads of lochs from which they could sail anywhere. Soon the old names were familiar to them – Lorn, Cowal, Knapdale, Kintyre, Appin, Morvern, Sunart. All of them had low hills to start on alongside the majestic peaks whose summits held views their clan ancestors had for centuries been dazed by. For those who sailed, there were the unrivalled coastal varieties of every kind of seascape, together with ample harbours and anchorages.

It was mainly unemployed miners who developed and popularised the great flush of angling which brought bands of men to all the rivers and inland lochs. You could see their camp-fires and hear their songs late at night in many a quiet spot. They were after food in the first place, and some of their activity was poaching, although a great many fishing areas were free. However, in the end they were forming fishing clubs with rules and conditions, and knowing the lifetime fever that affects people who take to the rod and the trout fly. They were not only attracted by the big rivers, the Etive, the Awe, the Orchy, the Strae, the Creran. There were also thousands of small burns cascading off the hills and every one of these – as can be seen from the older Ordnance Survey maps – had its Gaelic name, descriptive of the place and of an affectionate and vanished people who had endowed them in baptism.

There is not much big agriculture here. Like much of the western Highlands it is all sheep country and hill cattle. There are other evidences of industry of a sort; oysters and lobsters get good markets far afield. There is inshore and lochside fishing with visitors and the natives out in small boats, seeking the evening rise. And Argyll, of course, is clan country. You find here Macnaughtons, Macarthurs, Macgregors, Macdonalds, Macdougalls and, above all, the ascendant Campbells. Apart from the dukedom of Argyll, the place still bears the name of innumerable small Campbell lairdships, some of them holding long to the land. The enemies of the Campbells – and they had plenty – did not regard them as particularly a warlike clan although you do not capture a great part of the Highlands without having some skills in battle. Their critics used to say that they won most of their lands by the pen and not by the sword, indicating they knew some subtleties in the legal process which was denied in knowledge to the more rumbustious hill men. However, they wield the pen still with some effect, and there have been notable literary contributions from such as Inverneil and Kilberry, and even, at times, from Inveraray Castle itself.

In the cause of tradition, and more lately of industry, it should be mentioned at this point that the slogan cry of the Campbell clan is "Cruachan", the challenging shout of which raised their spirits in strenuous battlefields far away. For "Cruachan" is at the middle of their home territory, a splendid granite hill with several peaks which rises above Loch Awe. It plays a great part in the operations of the hydro-electric power schemes, because the vast caverns to accommodate the machinery and power plant of the installation have been hollowed out of its solid granite heart. It is a great exercise in conservation ingenuity – worth visiting. There are sites of older industries nearby, including the great spoil bings of what was an immensely important slate quarrying undertaking at Ballachulish. New roofing substitutes have come up to take the place of slates, just as new road surfaces have for long been taking over from the granite that used to pave roads many miles away from the hills whence it was hewn. An interesting, continuing symbol of the skilled quarrying of slate is to be seen in the graveyards of Ballachulish where many of the tombstones, carved in their lifetime, in many cases, by the grave's own occupants, still stand, neither mossy nor tilting after a century or more. I remember when the quarrymen used to have the raw slabs standing against the gable ends of their own homes, and they would work for a winter or two to shape and ornament the slab of slate that would eventually stand at their grave's head.

Another novelty is what used to be described as the only bridge across the Atlantic. It links the road from Oban to the island of Seil, and a rising and falling tide runs endlessly like a river below it. Nearby also is the disused railway bridge, now a one-way road track bearing the busy traffic to Benderloch. And now, if you are in a mood to be guided, don't fail to drive from end to end of our beloved Glen Orchy, the favourite of them all. It is beautiful in itself, and is especially endeared to us because, under one frail travelling roof or another, we have slept there many times, and followed quiet trails up the spendid hills, full of ruined clachans of those who have gone.

Argyll has many and many an island. Of these, I will mention only two here. The island of Gigha is off the west coast of Kintyre, and small as it is – less than 4,000 acres – it is a parish all by itself. Many a man would prefer to be the Laird of Gigha than the Duke of Sutherland. The highest hill is well under 300 feet and from the top you can see the whole place, green and sheltered by the sea.

Luing is about the same size as Gigha and it also packs into its small shape a huge bundle of what can best be described as scenery. It used to do a big trade in slate and sheep, with famous lobster fishing round its bitten coast. As has been said, the sea is everywhere.

This is more than you can say of Perthshire, which is so much an inland county away from the sea that many Scots feel as cut off from the sea when living in it, as they would in Missouri. But all the same it is a noble, and indeed a royal, county. To be sure the sea searches up the River Tay as far as the royal burgh of Perth, which has a harbour and no doubt a harbourmaster and almost certainly one or two harbour bars. There are fine parklands and all the hills and glens you could possibly want, and the rivers as well. The sight of the River Dochart hurrying through the wide rocky shallows to and under the Killin bridge from where it rushes to Loch Tay, is one of the most photographed scenes anywhere.

The Duke of Atholl, who is head of the Clan of Murray, lives in the county, much of which he owns. His castle is one of the most frequently visited in Scotland and he has some other tricks, like being the only man in Britain entitled to have his own private army (armed and with a pipe-band), to which it is a great county honour to belong. Famous piping contests are held in the castle under the Duke's auspices and Sir Yehudi Menuhin turns up from time to time to play his violin alongside the local fiddle band and to perfect his fingering of the "Scotch snap" in the strathspey. Surprises everywhere!

Sir Walter Scott used to say that Perthshire "forms the fairest portion of the northern kingdom – the most varied and the most beautiful" and certainly every corner of it is lovely and some are staggeringly so. It has its songs and poets too, of course, not least the poem that a certain Robertson made about the Marquis of Breadalbane at the very beginning of this century and which *Punch* thought funny enough to put into its columns, although it is perhaps doubtful if *Punch* would publish such a masterpiece today. It should be said that most of Perthshire was owned for many a day by the Marquis of Breadalbane, a very able Campbell offshoot who took that part of Perthshire and spread far and wide, owning, as Robertson said, pretty nearly everything. But he said it irresistibly:

Frae Kenmore to Ben Mhor
The land is a' the Marquis's,
The mossy howes, the heathery knowes,
and ilka bonny park is his.

The bearded goats, the touzy stots
and a' the braxy carcases;
The tinkers' tents, the crofters' rents
And ilka collie's bark is his.

The muircocks craw, the piper's blaw
The ghillie's hard day's wark is his.
Frae Kenmore to Ben Mhor
The warld is a' the Marquis's.

CASTLE STALKER AND LOCH LINNHE AT PORTNACROISH

WOODS NEAR PITLOCHRY, PERTHSHIRE

KYLES OF BUTE NEAR COLINTRAIVE

CULLIPOOL, LUING

BEN ARTHUR ('THE COBBLER')

GIGHA

BARLEY FIELD, GIGHA

OFFSHORE ISLANDS, LUING

LUING

FLOTSAM IN WEST TARBERT BAY, GIGHA

Ben Lomond and the Arrochar Hills

LOCH AWE AND BEINN A RHUIRIDH

LOCH SHIRA AND INVERARAY

LOCH AWE NEAR KILCHURN

GLEN TILT, PERTHSHIRE

LOCH ERICHT, PERTHSHIRE

LOCH RANNOCH, PERTHSHIRE

BEN MORE AND STOBINIAN, PERTHSHIRE

GLEN LYON, PERTHSHIRE

GLEN LYON, PERTHSHIRE

GARDENS AT ACHAMORE HOUSE, GIGHA

GLEN CROE AND BEN DONICH

FARM AT ARDLARACH, LUING

Luing school, june 1982

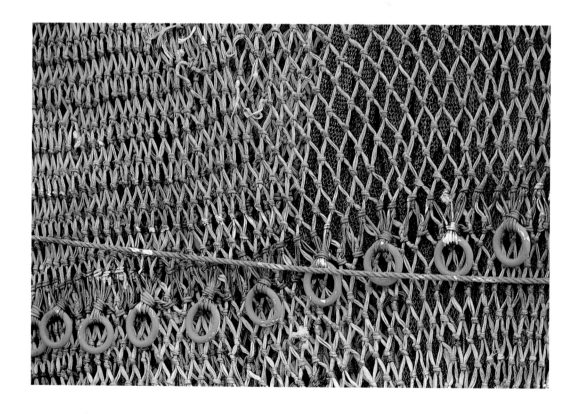

South pier, gigha

KILCHATTAN CHURCH-YARD, GIGHA

SOUTH PIER, GIGHA

GIGHA, LOOKING SOUTH, IN EARLY MORNING

RED DEER IN GLEN ORCHY

GULL CHICKS, LUING

SUNSET ON LOCH STRIVEN, COWAL, NEAR DUNOON

THE CENTRAL HIGHLANDS

Text by Alastair Dunnett Photographs by David Paterson

As you fare north from Argyll and Perthshire, you cross the county boundaries into the greatest of the Scottish counties – Inverness-shire. It is our largest, the most mountainous and the roughest as well as being one of the most sparsely inhabited. A solid and tremendous mass of mainland Scotland, yet it contains upwards of 20 islands where people still live and some of these are endearing places that no one would want to leave. Inverness-shire contains our greatest peaks, our greatest centre of whisky excellence, our saddest battlefield, our greatest rivers, our greatest triumphs of wildlife conservation and, perhaps most basic of all, our greatest variety of geology. For geology is almost exclusively a Scottish study – you might almost say a Scottish invention – because of the variety of the rocks and strange formations which all add up, again, to scenery.

These mountains and the glens carved out of them were not pushed up above the plains by any simple upheaval. They came out of the turmoil of the cooling world at widely different periods, some of the northern Highland rocks being about as old as any rocks in the world can be, while others are geological newcomers. Time and again the land was immersed under the waters for ages, with mountain layers building up under the surface by infinite laborious deposit of silt, pressing and firming itself. Other ridges poured molten from the burst heart of the earth and chilled into shapes of which the highest existing ranges are only the remnant fragments. Most of the Highland hills were formed by weathering down rather than by heaving up. At intervals there would be mountains eroding for unknown millions of years when, in some new writhing of the core, fresh mountain ranges would be contorted and folded over on top of them; or they would founder for an aëon in the sea and a new mountain range would be built upon them by the slow dropping specks of silt. In the long course of time the rocks settled down; the volcanoes died. Much later came the ice, and still no man had seen Scotland. Great glaciers covered the sea and land of the whole of northern Europe, receding and advancing again as the Arctic temperature rose and fell. The glaciers carried masses of rocks and sand with them to smother parts of the land when the final melting came. They diminished slowly, damming up and flooding glens so that, from sodden reservoirs, far underground, springs would flow for ever.

The ice left great wounds on the face of the land, although in the end nothing of itself remained. Upon hill slopes which form Glen Roy are three flat level highways, at different heights, running around the shoulders of the hills, engineered without a single gradient. Gaelic legend has long described them as hunting roads of the ancient kings, but they are the shores of a dammed up glacial lake which drained off in three stages, probably spending thousands of years at each stage.

The first people that we know anything about, and we don't know much, were the Picts. This is Pict land, and when in time the clans came along and took possession it became Cameron country; and there were also Frasers, Clan Ranald Macdonalds and many another. David Paterson elects to put even Rannoch Moor and the Black Mount into this range of varieties although they belong strictly to the southern counties. However, he is undoubtedly right, for on that far western group of hills and especially on the huge and desolate moor, wild with beauty as you can see from his pictures, untameable by man – the railway was floated across on bundles of brushwood – the Cairngorm mountains themselves begin to run north-east in a rising spine to the great peaks of Cairn Gorm, Cairn Toul and Braeriach, and the others which are shared with the adjacent county of Aberdeenshire.

Ben Nevis, which dominates the sky above Fort William, is a western outpost as well as being the highest British mountain. It dominates Lochaber country and the name of Lochaber sounds sweetly in the ears of those who belong to that ancient district. It does not always draw the same respect from its near neighbours. My old friend, Kate Sinclair, who farmed with her brother John in their late years in Balquhidder, was a senior nurse for some time in Fort William. She had a mind of her own and she once fell out fiercely with a doctor who thought he knew better. Eventually he burst out at her: "You're a dour, proud, Lochaber woman." "How dare you!" she stormed back at him, "I'm not. I'm a dour, proud Argyll woman."

Splitting the county of Inverness-shire almost in two is the Great Glen, an enormous crack in the earth's crust, containing three deep water lochs which were eventually joined up by the formation of the Caledonian Canal, now 165 years old. There are those who tell you that the Highlands do not really start until you have crossed the Great Glen going north and west. It may be true but there's still a treasury of glory on this side and much to find and be happy about. For example, there comes to mind the enormous industry of Scotch whisky whose main centre and perhaps main point of excellence, too, is the Spey Valley. Most peoples have experimented with distilling but, like the bagpipes and the tartans and many another item of quality, the Scots seem to have carried the art somewhat further than many of the copiers.

The distilling of whisky, being an ancient process, bears many mysteries accumulated in the endless ages of experiment. The men of the distilleries are tense and brooding craftsmen, intent upon their vigil and wary for the impalpable signs which mark the changes from stage to stage in the making. The process is not a mechanical one and there are few exact measurable elements in it. Even the distillers themselves, who have in their long skills secrets worth a fortune, will admit that beyond their precise items of wisdom there lie unfathomable ranges of mystery which they cannot explain nor predict, and which they are glad simply to watch for and take as they come.

Something of this quietude lies in the very atmosphere of distilleries. Most of them are located far from crowded towns, in the rolling scenery which is readily thought of when Scotland comes to the mind. They are always much larger than expected, but folded unobtrusively into the hills, with trees sometimes partially hiding the long, low, silent buildings and stores, whitewashed and roofed with black slates; for all their size, nothing like a factory or a mill. For their size, too, the distilleries are not jostling full of workers all blindly repeating some modern task. There are few about; but, again, they are the men of a craft, and each one of them is earning more for the trade balance of Britain than the individuals of any other industry to be found between Land's End and Shetland.

The distillery straddles running water, and this is the mainspring of the affair, for every factor in the making of whisky returns to the quality of the water. Welling across subterranean granite beds, seeping through the peat banks and the gravel, running in the sun downwards towards the sea, hundreds of these Scottish hill burns carry, at different parts along their small length, some secret of ultimate flavour which no chemist can detect. Not all burns have this fortunate way with them, and the favoured ones are well known. Maurice Walsh, who was an exciseman in Scotland, before he became a romantic novelist in Ireland, has described how "I knew one small town with seven distilleries and I knew an expert who could distinguish the seven by bouquet alone. These seven distilleries were in one mile of a Highland river; they used the same water, peat and malt, and the methods of brewing and distillation were identical, yet each spirit had its own individual bouquet."

There is nothing, I think, that can be added to the strange lore about the Loch Ness monster but you will hear and see plenty about it as you traverse the shores of the biggest loch in the Great Glen. The roads on both sides also divert into splendid glens which are tranquil but which have seen great bustling days. If you go north on the railway, you will see spots that can only be reached by strenuous personal tramping over hill ridges. At the foot of Loch Treig, for instance, where the railway is high above it, you will see a hill called Creag Ghuanach which is not the greatest of the hills by that far loch, but it is the scene of one of the greatest of the Gaelic hunters' songs. An English version:

Meet the morn there on Creag Ghuanach,
Day is born there out of twilight.
Hunt and horn there on Creag Ghuanach –
And the hungry years forgetting me.

See afar how Albyn's fertile,
Sun nor star knows no southland
Rich as are the verdant kingdoms
My eye rules from Ghuanach Creag.

Fair's the dawn and fair's the noon day,
There's the Creag delights the hunter,
Cares are gone – but where are the comrades
Aye were with me on Ghuanach Creag?

I can leave age to timing,
To the grey bards their rhyming;
Joy's the day I'll be climbing
In the white cloud on Ghuanach Creag.

There are modern adventures for the adventurous. For a number of years Dorothy and I roamed away to the far north-west and elsewhere on horseback. One year it was robust Highland ponies, great beasts on the hill, plodders and amblers for ever and a day, but reluctant to canter or gallop. We wandered for a week or two through the moorish hinterland between the Moray Firth and the Mearns, finding amazing old and firm roads among the windings of the upland farm lands, and coming down at night only when it was time to look for a bed and horse park. After a day or two away from their known territory the beasts would not let us out of their sight, presumably since we were the only ones who would eventually take them home, and when we lunched or slept we let them wander, even with the saddle-bags open and all our gear ready to spill. It went wrong only on one day of low cloud when we were in the Abernethy Forest not far from the shores of the Green Loch. For half an hour or so, above us, there had been the intermittent sound of a small aircraft, probably feeling his way to Kinloss or Dyce, and we paid small attention. Suddenly this aerial fellow dived through the clouds, and came out a few hundred feet above us. Clearly he was lost, and took this desperate measure to locate himself. He must have spotted the terrain and the directions at once, for he bounced up through the cloud cover and disappeared somewhere in a beeline. But the horses had never seen anything like this and they took to their heels faster than they had ever gone under our direction. We went panting after them full speed through the high tripping heather, gathering up in the pursuit the costly items of clothing, binoculars, spare sweaters, whisky flasks, and other treasures which jolted out of the bags as they fled.

We got to love these horses too. They were as affectionate as dogs, although I do not suppose they even recognised their own names. Also, like us, they dearly loved chicken sandwiches. Horses are charming creatures, patient and submissive, and altogether noble. I do not understand why they can tolerate humans at all, far less allow themselves to be taken advantage of in the way they do.

If you haven't got songs or poetry to cheer your way, you can resort to reciting the stylish list of the rivers with their poetic names – Cannich, Farrar, Ness, Moriston, Garry, Spean; and a fuller version of an epic would be the names of the 100 good-sized lochs to be found in Inverness-shire alone, as well as the innumerable small ones, all named and ready for you.

The remote village of Applecross marks the north-western bounds of our territory. It is exactly 60 miles due west of Inverness on the opposite coast, and its situation is spectacular. This charming place looks out upon the island of Raasay and the mountains of Skye – "as fair a view as any in Scotland". Until recently you couldn't get to Applecross unless by sea or by climbing the formidable Bealach nam Ba, an apologetic motor road which climbs to over 2,000 feet and has hair-raising zig-zag turns. But there is now a new coast road round to Shieldaig. For that view, it demands to be taken.

LOCH QUOICH AND BENGAIRICH, INVERNESS-SHIRE

ROCK-FORMS, GLEN ETIVE

Sgurr an lochain and loch cluanie, west inverness-shire

GLEN ETIVE

LANDSCAPE, GLEN ETIVE

NORTH FACE BEN NEVIS, GREEN GULLY

SUN-UP IN GLEN NEVIS

'THE LOST VALLEY' GLENCOE, WITH BEN NEVIS AND THE MAMORE FOREST

BIVOUAC SHELTER, SUMMIT OF BEN NEVIS

WOODS, STRATHERRICK, INVERNESS-SHIRE

SGURR NA SGINE AND THE SADDLE, GLEN SHIEL

GLENQUOICH FOREST

GLENCOE AND LOCH ACHTRIOCHTAN

SRON NA CREISE, BUCHAILLE ETIVE MOR

STOB COIRE NAN LOCHAN, AT DUSK, GLENCOE

RANNOCH MOOR

BLACK MOUNT, RANNOCH MOOR

MEALL A BHUIRIDH, BLACK MOUNT, RANNOCH

COIRE AN LOCHAN, WESTERN CAIRNGORMS

Kinloch-hourn and sgurr a mhaoraich, inverness-shire

BLACK MOUNT, RANNOCH MOOR

Loch garry

KINCRAIG CHURCH, SPEY VALLEY

BEALACH NAM BA, APPLECROSS

MEALL GORM, APPLECROSS

SGURR A CHAORACHAIN, APPLECROSS

CLACH LEATHAD, BLACK MOUNT, RANNOCH

RIVER SHIEL AT SHIEL BRIDGE

THE FIVE SISTERS, KINTAIL

RIVER SHIEL AT SHIEL BRIDGE, INVERNESS-SHIRE

RUINS, NEAR AVIEMORE

THE ISLANDS

Text by Alastair Dunnett Photographs by David Paterson

The day will be sweet when at last I can go to you,
then all the seas of the islands I'll show to you,
Then I shall sing all the songs that I know to you,
There in the Islands of Glory.

Of these islands Skye is of course the pride and the gem. To people like me, when we talk of Skye we talk of sailing. And we shall come to that here, but do not be put off, for Skye is a great piece of splendour in its own right and it absorbs many a devotee who has a car or a bike or a good pair of legs; and it has fine roads and mountains that will take all that they want to expend. It is a big place, 50 miles long from north to south and well over 20 miles at its broadest, so it's bigger in itself than many a Scottish county. There are one or two ferry ways of getting to it by road and then by sea, but the handiest is the very narrow strait between Kyle of Lochalsh on the mainland and Kyleakin with the car and passenger ferry which crosses every few minutes, and even through the night from time to time. This is the calf country of most of the MacLeods and a great number of the Macdonalds.

Skye is most people's favourite island because it is so undoubtedly a place apart. If you were put down in any remote corner of it and asked to guess where you were, you would know that you certainly were on an island and that it wore a cloak of mystery and sorrows and romance (we've plenty of that) and arousal. It has a bustling town called Portree with a busy harbour where yachts and passenger craft come and there is shelter from all the storms. At the harbour roadside are congenial little places to eat and drink and have foregatherings of a neighbourly sort; while it has a social season with big-scale balls and dances and much entertainment.

There is also a township called Broadford which explains itself. For the most part, as you work your way round the coast, you will find that the names are once more into Viking country because these fellows called all the coastal strips and the landfalls by names which described them in their own tongue and made it easy for followers to recognise them. In the western parts also they came ashore and set up farmsteads and wintering places. The Norse and the Gaelic names compete all round although in the end it is the Gaelic names and the Gaelic people which have prevailed.

H. V. Morton, when he wrote about the Western Isles, described his disappointment in the Cuillin Hills – not the mountains themselves, which are amazing, but the name. He spelt it Coolins which he described as being a tame name more suitable for some semi-detached villa in the suburbs of London. However, he was a well-meaning Englishman and all his writings make deference to the sorcery of our places. These precipitous rocks, with 15 peaks over 3,000 feet, form an amazing view from any angle. They·have been the training ground of some of the best of the British climbers and a few of them were not even scaled until the lifetime of people still alive.

I have been in among them myself many times, but not with rope and axe. On my very first visit to Skye I had a weird experience in their shadow. From the hotel at Sligachan, for many years the great centre for angling and mountaineering on Skye, I planned to walk through the Cuillin Pass to Camasunary, a lone farmhouse on a bay in Loch Scavaig. The kindly owners had given a warmhearted welcome to a friend of mine when he pitched his tent alone in their neighbourhood. Their way of living, or his account of it, drew me. I shouldered my pack and set off past the foothills of Glamaig, with Marsco and Blaven looming on my left; at last I reached the top of the ridge which led me to the sea, and the fresh smell of the salt and the seaweed. From there, the farmhouse was in sight, but there was no smoke from the chimneys and, as I neared, no sound of sheep, or dogs barking. I knocked on the door, and then peered in the windows. In two rooms, bedclothes were thrown back as if the sleepers had roused and risen abruptly. A table was set for a meal that had been abandoned. I gave a few shouts, but the only reply was a misty echo, perhaps from as far as the slopes of Sgurr Alasdair. It seemed like a place claimed by disaster. It was not. Next day, after an uneasy night in a barn, I climbed out over the hills of the Strathaird Peninsula and down to the sparsely housed road round Loch Slapin. There I was told the story. The Camasunary family had left to take another farm in the south, but had been roused before time by the steam puffer come to transfer them. Their belongings in due course would follow. From time to time, I still glimpse the Camasunary house from the sea or from Elgol; but I have never been back.

I've been to most other places, though, including Dunvegan Castle, in the days when the modern Flora MacLeod was in residence. In due course she became both Dame and the Chief of her family, and it fell to me to pay tribute at her 90th birthday. Dorothy tells some of the tales of Dunvegan, but I like to recall the MacCrimmons, hereditary pipers to the Clan MacLeod, who had a famous piping school here, dispensing training in all the deep skills of that musical art. The family of MacLeod are still in residence.

In Skye, there are a thousand cunning places to anchor. Once we put down to the north-west in the lee of Tulm Island, and spent an evening with old friend and naturalist Seton Gordon. Seton, an ornithologist and historian, a judge of piping and a kilt-wearing Scot who lived to a great age, turns up more than once in my story. A fine hill man, too. When I saw him a year or two later he said that he had climbed some rise after our meeting, and watched with his telescope our passage from Rubha Hunish across the Minch to Rodel in Harris.

Skye has also got its little islands. South Rona, off the coast, near Staffin, is deserted and I think even the lighthouse keepers have gone; but it has one or two fine anchorages, including one whose Gaelic name means simply "the big anchorage", with a dodgy entrance and some helpful signs on which yachtsmen have inscribed notices indicating the course towards the inland sheltered part. I tell you, you don't get many signposts when you are at sea, but this is quite a place. You could then walk to where the old village was, with houses still standing and the church almost intact even now, with the open bibles left at salient passages.

To the south of Skye lies the Parish of the Small Isles, much loved by David Paterson as you can tell from his photographs. Rhum is a quite beautiful island, long since cleared of the people who named every stream and brae face and were happy there. It must be that New Zealand and Canada and such places are the richer for Scotland's clearance, but the place they left behind became an island where no visitors were wanted and indeed were repelled.

Dorothy mentions Kinloch Castle in her essay. Long before I was married, friend James Adam and I landed on Rhum with our canoes, to camp for the night, and were made to understand the nature of the privacy required by the new laird and his people. The time was the Depression and we were far from being tourists, having set out on a trip by single-seater canoes from the Clyde to the Outer Hebrides as a means of drawing attention, by our reports and our writings, to the unhappy social state of the Highlands and isles among which we were travelling. The trip became celebrated, and perhaps some ills were righted because of it. We were not, however, in a state to be impressed by the excesses of Sir George Bullough's marble-filled edifice, or still less by his electric roll-playing organ, with its full drum-kit and flutes enabling *Cavalleria Rusticana* to thunder through the still (and exclusive) Highland air of the island.

Nearby is Eigg, like a ship's prow riding south towards the gales. Its unmistakable cliff points into the wind. Here, too, successive lairds have ventured to change the way of life of the remaining inhabitants, but you can still

THE ISLANDS

go there if you plan your own travelling. Further south lies a great island, rivalled only by Skye in the inner seas. Mull has had a lively lifestyle for all the time I have known it. There is a small fishing harbour called Tobermory about which Harry Lauder used to sing a song with little Gaelic authenticity. As well as his civic duties, its recent provost Bobby MacLeod ran one of the very best dance bands in existence. A fragment of rock and land off Mull's south-western end is Iona, our sacred island, of which Dorothy speaks. The Cathedral there was a ruin until our own lifetime when it was restored, roofed, and has become an ecumenical church where all of Christian faith are welcome.

We now leap to the Outer Isles, across the stormy Minch which has shaken many a hardy seafarer. These form a string of islands 140 miles long, and are as often as not called "The Long Island". The Atlantic rollers beat on every west shore. The most northerly and largest and probably the most prosperous, is the island of Lewis whose capital is Stornoway. Townships and an assortment of ribbon-built houses run along the roads right to the north. Lewis is joined to Harris by land, although they tend to be thought of as separate islands. The world-famous Harris tweed is made in both places, although the smell of peat and dye-lichens no longer dwells in the nose.

On the east side, where geological disturbance anciently raised the land, remain the small harbours and fishing communities; while all down the west coast, where the land was once dipped into the sea, are endless beaches of dazzling white sand. Dorothy has spoken of the chill of the water. I can endorse it.

It's a Gaelic-speaking area, all of this Long Island, although everybody speaks English as well. For historical reasons the northern half of the Outer Hebrides tends to subscribe to the Presbyterian faith, while the southern half is devotedly Catholic. Yet it is a good unity; and friendly to visit. Cars can be taken to most parts of it, and at some points bridges cross waterways. In the middle of the belt are the islands of South and North Uist and Benbecula and there are fragments of inhabited isles in between, with their own boats for fishing and visiting. Then there is miraculous Barra, with its lively and mischievous people, its primrose fields and its beaches. Sir Compton Mackenzie made it one of his island homes – his other, in these parts, lay in the Shiant Isles, where now the sea rolls unregarded on the great fossil stones of the beaches, and the puffins stand on the slopes undisturbed.

You anchor at Barra off Castlebay. On the small island offshore is Kisimul Castle, the ancient headquarters of the Clan MacNeil, which lay in ruins

110

for centuries until the prospective chief of the Clan – reared in America – determined to restore it, and had himself trained as an architect in order to do so. To the end of his life, Robert MacNeil crossed the Atlantic each summer to see his work progress, until the castle was fit to be lived in, and he could hold his first banquet, and have his piper proclaim from the battlements: *"Hear oh ye people, and listen oh ye nations! The great MacNeil of Barra having finished his meal, the princes of the earth may now dine."*

Barra's airport is a stretch of two miles of firm white sand which, unlike most airports in the world, is covered by the tide twice a day. But who would fly while he can sail? Although it takes a stout sailor to make for St. Kilda.

I have a special feeling for the group of islands known as St. Kilda, which lie out in the Atlantic, 45 miles west of North Uist. I am one of the few people who knew the islands in 1930, while men and women and children still lived there. In that year, the remaining population were taken off, because there were too few able men for survival. In later years, Dorothy and I had the privilege many times of landing on St. Kilda under National Trust for Scotland auspices, conducting parties along the single street of deserted small houses, and climbing dizzying cliffs to see the seabirds and seals far below. It is a wild place to reach and to anchor in, because the village bay faces south-west where the gales come from, and they get up fast. But, over the years, work parties from the Trust have rebuilt and repaired the old village, made safe the church, and cut the grass in the graveyard so that it remains a seemly monument, but it is strange to see the empty hearths where people have stayed in my lifetime.

GRIBUN HEAD AND LOCH NA KEAL, MULL

CALLANISH, LEWIS

SHEEP SHEARING, BUNESSAN, MULL

BEN BUIE, MULL

BALMEANACH AND CREAG A' CHAILL, MULL

DEAD CORMORANT, UIG BAY, SKYE

LOCH DHUGAILL AND THE COULINS, SKYE

MACLENNAN'S STORES, RAASAY, AUGUST 1982

NORTH HARBOUR, SCALPAY

BROCHEL CASTLE, RAASAY

HALLIVAL AND BARKEVAL, RHUM

THE GREAT HALL, KINLOCH CASTLE, RHUM

THE MAUSOLEUM, HARRIS GLEN, RHUM

RHUM FROM SKYE

STORNOWAY, LEWIS

LOCH BRITTLE AND GLEN BRITTLE, SKYE

SOUND OF SLEAT AT ARMADALE, SKYE

VATERSAY BAY, VATERSAY

TARSKAVAIG AND THE COULINS, SKYE

LORD MACDONALD'S FOREST, GLAMAIG, SKYE

GRESHORNISH, NORTHERN SKYE

LOCH BRACADALE, WEST COAST OF SKYE

BORVE, BARRA

LOCH SLAPIN WITH BLAVEN AND CLACH GLAS, SKYE

ORD, LOCH EISHORT, SKYE

CASTLEBAY, BARRA

STAC LEE, ST KILDA

GLEN DRYNOCH AND THE COULINS, SKYE

SGURR ALASDAIR, THE COULINS

GLEN BRITTLE, SKYE

LOCH DHUGAILL AND THE COULINS, SKYE

THE NORTH
AND WEST HIGHLANDS

Text by Alastair Dunnett Photographs by David Paterson

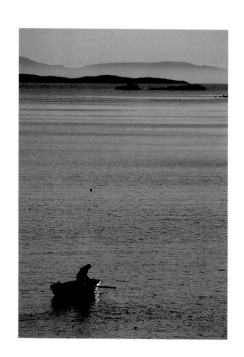

I HAVE SPENT A LIFETIME OF WRITING ABOUT SCOTLAND WHILE VAINLY trying to eliminate all traces of prejudice or historical preference. Even so, I hope I may be forgiven a small portion of my inoffensive bias in stating some sort of prejudice for this most northern part of our area, especially Caithness, where half of me springs from. Indeed, I even go overseas at that point because my male side of the northern genealogy comes from the island of Stroma, where my great-grandfather farmed the whole island, living in the splendid house, now ruined, of Stroma Mains, and he might well have been described as laird of the place. When the Crofters Acts were passed in the late 1880s he was bought out so that the authorities could turn the island into a crofting scene for a score or two of crofts, with seemly houses and a settled population, and my forefather came to farm around the area of the large farms of Canisbay which flanked the Castle of Mey. Time has gone on and there are no permanent residents at all on the Island of Stroma.

The people of Caithness would not thank you for calling them Highland. They imagine themselves to be of pure Norse descent, although my own father in appearance and style had no resemblance to anyone I see around present-day Scandinavia. But I spent a piece of my boyhood in Caithness, and got a feeling for these windswept boggy plains that run from the great inland hills down to the sea to end in precipitous cliffs, or in great sandy bays and beaches where the sandstone has been ground to a pink powder.

It has uses. The Dounreay people, for example, have set up sand-yachting excitements in the pure and glorious curve of Dunnet Bay. Such a sport is new to the area, and so are the people. They come from the nuclear establishment whose huge metal globe interrupts the flat, treeless landscape near Thurso. Atomic research has brought there a whole generation of incoming boffins, and with them their sports and hobbies to revive some of the old literary and debating societies in which Caithness was once prolific.

What draws me still to Caithness are the older things. All mortals find themselves warm to one or two particular spots and, even in small Scotland, there are too many places upon which one can lavish the entire affection born of one's inheritance. So we select – and there's no harm in that. This is no more than photographers do. They are brought to dwell on some place, not only because of its visual perfection as they see it, but from some instinct of heart or of heritage. It was Rudyard Kipling who said – and he was a great English poet with a Highland grandmother, which all decent Englishmen are anxious to claim –

God gave all men all earth to love,
And since our hearts are small,
Ordained for each, one spot should prove
Beloved over all.

For some, Sutherland calls in this way. It is quite different from Caithness. Here we are back in a mountainous county, and a wide and wild one. It stretches from the Atlantic Ocean to the North Sea, with a great scattering of high hills and lochs and bogs, with roads wending in amongst them, or diving inland to follow the coastline round the deep bays. There are a few sheltered glens eagerly cultivated but, on the whole, the country is more suited for sheep than folk, and the population is sparse indeed. Mixed with Gaelic, Scandinavian names remain from the Norse days – among them Cape Wrath, which at the extreme north-west juts into the ocean. Its name has nothing to do with wrath or tumult of the seas, although they are fierce enough. The name means "turning-point", where seafaring men in their galleys rounded the corner and turned south to the rich pickings of Irish and Scottish settlements. There are no western towns, but a fine coastline there and a great scattering of splendid little islands. The towns are on the east coast, facing the North Sea. Dornoch is the old county town, famous for its cathedral and, of course, for its golf course of championship quality, the Royal Dornoch, where the game has been played for 360 years. Not far away is Brora which had the oldest coal mine in Scotland and which has dabbled in one industry or another.

I never leave Sutherland without paying tribute to a group of hills in the far south-west. Canisp and Suilven are talked of whenever delectable mountains are named. They rise in isolation from the plain and they look across the old county boundary to Cul Mor and Cul Beag which stand in the north part of Wester Ross. This was once a mountain chain, long years ago weathered down into these fine monuments. Their tops can be reached by a strenuous walk.

Wester Ross. Now that's the place! It's probably the favourite location of all for those who come from far away once in a while, to walk the hills and breathe the air and listen to the endless sound of water, or simply stand in a daze to look. The geological history of Wester Ross is what gives it its amazing variety of scenes that people will remember long after, and photographers strive to make immortal. There is virtually nothing here but hills and rivers and lochs and, in the old times, Mackenzies. But the sea creeps in upon it all down the west side, embracing the headlands that thrust out. These peninsulas have roads of a sort, leading well into them, and it's no great hardship, when the road ends, to walk the rest of the way to the cliff edge where there are lighthouses. This rugged and noble territory was once covered with natural forest but these have gone, and there are indeed few trees, except those forested along the lower roads.

Not many people can live off the land, so they have in most cases taken to the sea, with inshore fishing and, of course, the lobsters. There is also fishing on a somewhat larger scale. Ullapool is a large village which was especially built for the fishing industry 200 years ago and it is the headquarters now of great fleets of fishing vessels. Waiting offshore to buy and process the catches are factory ships of many nations, some of them from beyond the Iron Curtain, with their native crews. These Russians and Poles and others come ashore to stock up with local food and drink, and also to make purchases of such items as are in short supply in their own countries, like radios and television sets, stereos, recorders, computers, calculating machines and other gadgets, immense supplies of which have been shrewdly put into stock by the local shopkeepers who may one day look back on these years as boom times. The same offshore activity with foreign fleets can be seen at Kinlochbervie, another thriving fishing port away in the north near Cape Wrath. On the narrow road leading south from Kinlochbervie you may have to jostle with enormous refrigerator vans bustling south to markets with part of the catch. You would be wise to pull into a passing place and let them thunder on.

There is a mountain in Wester Ross which is specially dear to me. Ben Mor Coigach heaves up sharply from the sea at the entrance to Loch Broom and I climbed it one memorable day in the company of Michael Powell, the film producer, Bill Paton and Seton Gordon as well as Alick Bartholomew, one of the map family. I carried Seton Gordon's pipes up from the shores of Loch Lurgain and when we got on the top and had a breather, Seton played his pipes memorably, giving us two splendid pibrochs and a number of other more frivolous items. It was a sunny day, wonderfully clear, and that great hill-man pointed out the innumerable peaks we could see. Away to the west like a long, low cloud was the string of the Outer Hebrides on the horizon. He identified for us the flat top of Dun Caan in Raasay over 50 miles away.

Dougie, Seton's dog, went with us to every top on that trip and no dog ever had a gentler master. It was among these hills at that time that I came to realise that Seton was getting frail at last and was also getting very deaf. He would spot some small distant bird with his binoculars and then whistle its song, saying to us, "Is that what that bird is singing?" and if it was so, he would tell us its

145

name. The last I saw of Seton on that trip was in his hotel room when, having an early start the next morning, I went in to say good-bye. He didn't hear me coming and he was kneeling on the floor in his old kilt, holding a tumblerful of water from which Dougie was lapping, there being no dog dish.

I have also walked a precipitous path along the west face of Ben Mor Coigach, and across Strath Kanaird by Ardmair to Ullapool. The foothills of Ben Mor Coigach run down to Achiltibuie from whose little harbour you go to the Summer Isles. Here again, is a group upon which our photographer dotes. The biggest one is Tanera More which was the home for some years of Sir Frank Fraser Darling, the outstanding ecologist who wrote classic books about the problems and the natural resources of the remote west Highland places. Darling became the director of the West Highland Survey and his books remain standard works. The Summer Isles run outwards toward the sea in a little string with Tanera Beg nestling near the big one and Priest Island, to take the English name of this ancient hermit's refuge, being the last. As the sea opens up, you go round Greenstone Point and then Rudha Reidh and then south to Gairloch and beyond – if you must go south.

Dorothy and I were in at the very beginning of pony trekking in the north and west Highlands and the phrase itself was, I believe, invented by our old friend, Jock Kerr Hunter. It started in the Highlands because Ewan Cameron, the hotel keeper and impresario of hunting and stalking in the Highlands – he used to be the go-between in renting shoots and stalks for wealthy visitors – had a large herd of Highland ponies which used to carry the slain game down from the hills, from carcases of deer over their backs to baskets containing grouse and game of all descriptions. These are willing animals, used to the hill tracks and as they say, sure-footed. Jock and he thought up the idea of a scheme to use the animals for teaching novices to ride and to enjoy the glens and hill tracks that abound in the moorland areas of Scotland. Jock, Howard Paterson, Dorothy and I spent a weekend "riding in" some of the ponies and plotting out some of the earliest pony-trekking circuits around Ewan's base at Newtonmore. This was the start of it all.

For a year or two after that Dorothy and I spent our holidays in this way, not around the doors of Newtonmore, but far afield with horses and saddlebags of clothes and other gear. We went as far as Lochinver in the west and the Moray uplands in the east, staying in small hotels or farmhouses with an adjacent field for the ponies. In these early days it was a study to notice how enthusiastic the country people were about horses. Most of them, even on the smaller farms, had given up horses and had taken to tractors, and when they heard us coming they would straggle to the gates or the road-end just to talk about the horses. It's a good way of getting to know people. The knowledgable ones often will not address you for a moment or two, but will seize the horse's muzzle and pull open its mouth to look at its teeth. Some sort of introduction generally follows.

In the north and west, as in almost all parts of the Scottish Highlands, there's some good music going and lots of good conversation. Every second person is a poet and everyone is a singer. There's a jaunty Gaelic song about the joy there is in taking the High Road. An English version goes:

> *Here's a song for days of spring,*
> *Here's a road for wandering,*
> *Where's the man that canna sing*
> * On the road to Albyn.*

> *Sure in sun and rain we'll go*
> *Sure we'll put the miles below,*
> *Joy is surely their's who know,*
> * Every road in Albyn.*

> *Summer kiss of winds we'll meet,*
> *Where the peaks the dawning greet,*
> *Put the clouds below our feet*
> * On the hills of Albyn.*

Albyn is of course one of the old Gaelic names for Scotland. It's a great place to visit and come back to and the Highlands are for many the most joyous place on earth. People bring tents and caravans and there are endless facilities for these. Others find rooms in cottages and farmhouses. There are many splendid hotels, and the great upgrading of the small hotel and the pub lunch. The roads are better than they have ever been and emptier than most roads anywhere. Even the single track ones with passing places are perfectly manageable and there's usually an agreeable surprise around every bend. What more could you ask for?

THE SUMMER ISLES SEEN FROM POLBAIN ON THE MAINLAND

AN TEALLACH AND THE GARBH ALLT

ESTUARY OF RIVER FLEET, LITTLE FERRY, SUTHERLAND

MOONRISE OVER CANISP, SUTHERLAND

DRIFT NETTING IN ACHMELVICH BAY, NEAR LOCH INVER

ACHNAHEARD, WESTER ROSS

ACHILTIBUIE AND STAC POLLY

LOCH AT SANDWOOD, SUTHERLAND

STAC POLLY WITH CUL MOR, ASSYNT HILLS

A SUNSET FROM TANERA MORE, SUMMER ISLES

TANERA MORE, SUMMER ISLES WITH ACHILTIBUIE AND THE ASSYNT HILLS

HELMSDALE AND THE HELMSDALE RIVER, SUTHERLAND

LOCH GLENDHU AND QUINAG, SUTHERLAND

SUMMIT OF QUINAG, SUTHERLAND

DIABEG, WESTER ROSS

BEN GRIAM, CAITHNESS AND SUTHERLAND BORDERS

CAITHNESS COAST, NEAR BERRIEDALE

THE BLACK ISLE, INVERNESS-SHIRE

LIATHACH AND UPPER LOCH TORRIDON, WESTER ROSS

Ferns in autumn, Inverness-shire

ACHMELVICH, NEAR LOCHINVER

LOCH SHIN, SUTHERLAND

Cul mor, central sutherland

SUILVEN, SUTHERLAND

GAIRLOCH, WESTER ROSS

KINLOCHBERVIE, SUTHERLAND

SUILVEN AND WESTER ROSS FROM QUINAG

LOCH MORE, SUTHERLAND

DAWN OVER NORTHERN SUTHERLAND FROM BEN KLIBRECK

DAWN OVER CENTRAL SUTHERLAND AND CAITHNESS

BEINN DAMPH FOREST, WESTER ROSS